APRIL · MAY · JUNE

Pisces · Aries · Taurus
$\mathcal{H}$ Υ $\bm{\aleph}$

Spring

Virgo · Libra · Scorpio
$\bm{\mathfrak{M}}$ $\bm{\Omega}$ $\bm{\mathfrak{M}}$

Autumn

OCTOBER · NOVEMBER · DECEMBER

The Story of
Our Calendar

The Story of
Our Calendar

by RUTH BRINDZE

Illustrations by

HELENE CARTER

THE VANGUARD PRESS, INC.
New York

Eighth Printing

Contents

Sky Time

Do you know that the calendar is in the sky? Few people do. They think of a calendar as a commonplace thing made of paper or of cardboard, but the real calendar is in the sky, and this was discovered thousands of years ago. It was the first great scientific discovery.

The calendar we use is so simple and so easy to understand that it is hard to believe men had to work for thousands of years before they discovered how to put together days, weeks, months, and years. And it is also hard to believe that long ago calendars were even kept secret.

There is much to tell about how our calendar started, how it was changed and improved. How ancient men kept track of time according to the moon, which is the reason our calendar is divided into moons, or months. And then, how scientists who lived long ago learned to use the sun as a yearly clock, which is the reason our calendar is kept according to sun years. Counting a certain number of days as a week is another division of time established by the skygazers of long ago.

All sorts of mistakes were made before the ancient scientists devised a calendar system that was nearly right. For example, at one period extra months had to be added every so often to fill out a year. Imagine the inconvenience of never knowing whether there would be twelve or thirteen months to a year!

There are tales of the calendar mix-up in the kingdom of Babylonia, where a new month was begun after each new crescent moon, and of what happened in Egypt when the calendar-makers tried the simple system of dividing a year into months of exactly 30 days. There are other stories about the Romans, who gave the calendar its name, and of why, even now, today's date is different in different parts of the world. For instance, at this very moment it is one day later in Australia than it is in the United States.

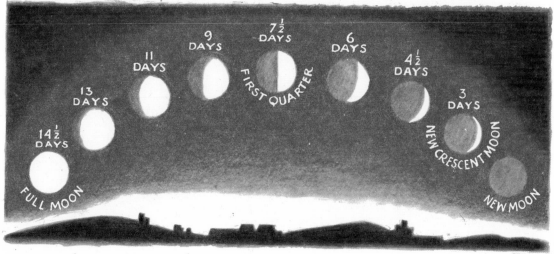

People living in every part of the world — in the South Sea Islands and in China, in ancient Egypt and in Mexico — have made calendars according to the stars and the moon and the sun.

But the calendar we use got its start in ancient Egypt, and in the neighboring kingdom called Babylonia, where men were especially skilful at skygazing. Long before there were any civilized nations in Europe, Egypt and Babylonia were great countries where all sorts of scientific work was carried on.

Word about the calendars used by the Egyptians and the Babylonians was carried from one country to another by travelers and businessmen and soldiers, just as today people who have visited other countries talk of what they have seen. In this way information about calendars was carried to Europe. And after powerful nations were established there, the scientists and the rulers of these nations copied the ideas that seemed to fit their needs. Thousands of years later, when English and European colonists sailed for America, they brought with them the calendars they had used in their homelands. So the system for keeping track of time developed by the Egyptians, by the Babylonians, and by other ancient scientists took hold in the new world.

To know the real story behind the neat little calendars we use today, we must find out how the very ancient people made their timetables according to the stars and the moon and the sun. We must travel from country to country to learn how calendars were changed and improved. It is an exciting expedition.

Counting Moons

KING HAMMURABI had just returned to his palace when he heard the new moon signal. He heard it clearly, for the king's residence in Babylon was just across the square from the big temple, the one with the tallest tower in the city. It was from this tower that the high priest, who was also the official calendar maker, would watch the heavens as the sun was setting, and at the first sight of the new moon he would blow his horn.

In the kingdom of Babylonia, a new month was begun when a new moon was seen, and one of the high priest's duties was to keep a regular lookout for the crescent moon. Soon after giving this new-moon signal, he walked down from the tower and crossed over to the palace where he reported to the king.

"This is going to be a thirteen-month year," he said. "The people should be so informed."

Hammurabi had made many improvements in the laws, and in the other affairs of his country. But he never had tried to regulate the calendar. He would not have dared to do this because, like other Babylonians, he believed the moon was a god. If the moon-god caused a mix-up of the calendar, it just had to be accepted.

11

"The sooner the people get the news, the better it will be," he thought, so he called for the royal scribe and dictated the following message:

"This month is Elulu. The coming month shall therefore be called 2nd Elulu."

The king pressed his royal seal into the soft clay on which the message had been written (kings did not sign their names to letters or to anything else in those days), and messengers were dispatched to the governors of the important cities of Babylonia. Some of these messengers rode off on donkeys, but many messengers traveled by boat, for there were numerous rivers and canals in the kingdom, and water travel was easy and fast.

News that there was to be an extra month spread quickly, and, even though Babylonians were accustomed to such changes, many merchants grumbled and complained. Those who expected to collect bills at the end of the year grumbled the most, for now they would have to wait an extra month to collect their money.

The reason for Babylonia's calendar trouble was that, although the months were figured according to the moon, the year was measured according to the sun.

Now, there are only a little more than 29 days between new moons (this is how long it takes the moon to travel around our planet, the earth, and to be visible again as a thin crescent). But the sun year is a little more than 365 days. The two systems of moon months and sun year could not be made to fit together evenly, so every once in a while an extra month had to be added to round out a year.

The high priest was a first-rate scientist, and he knew how to measure a sun year. He could do this without any special instruments. All he needed was a single stake, or marker, driven firmly into the ground. He used this marker to measure the sun's position at the moment it appeared on the horizon at dawn.

The high priest had been taught by older priests how to do this; the method had been known for a long time. At sunrise he would stand directly behind the marker, facing the sun, and on most mornings he would see the sun rise a little to one side or the other of the marker. But there were special mornings when the sun appeared on a direct line with the marker, or exactly in the east. These were the days for which the high priest watched, for they were celebrated as holidays in Babylonia.

We call these days the *equinoxes,* and there is one about March 21 and another about September 23. On these days the hours of daylight and of darkness are equal.

The Babylonian scientists kept careful records of the number of times they saw the sun rise directly in back of the marker. Each time, according to their calendar system, marked the end of half a year.

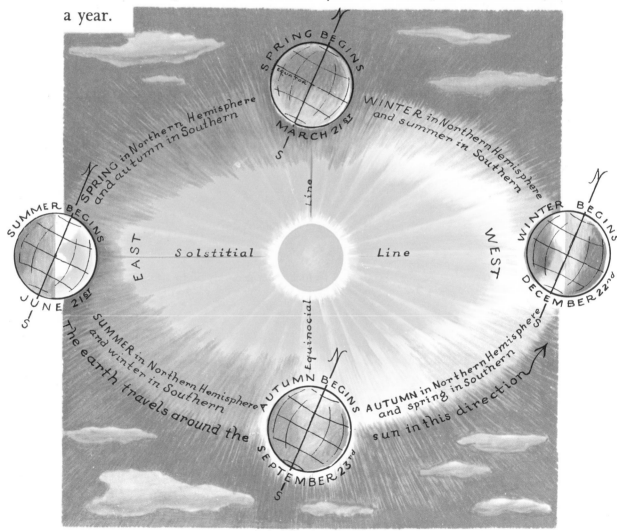

Of course, they did not know the scientific reason for the equinoxes. They could not possibly have known the reason, because the Babylonians believed that the sun and the stars revolved around the earth. We know that the equinoxes occur because the earth travels around the sun and because the earth's axis is tilted. As our planet, the earth, makes its round-the-sun journey, the north pole is sometimes closer to the sun than the south pole. But twice during this annual journey the north pole and the south pole are exactly the same distance from the sun. This happens on the days that we call the equinoxes.

In Babylonia, one of these days was celebrated as the New Year's holiday, the most exciting of the year. There was a great parade in which Hammurabi and other state officials took part, and as boys and girls and grown-ups watched from the side lines, venders of sweets made of honey and nuts passed through the crowds, just as peddlers do nowadays with popcorn, candies, and soda.

Why didn't the Babylonians keep their calendar by the sun alone? There are many possible explanations: First, the moon is a convenient timekeeper, since it appears, grows, and disappears at such regular, and short, intervals; secondly, the Babylonians thought that the moon-god was more important than the sun-god and wished to give it first place. They thought that the moon was the father of the sun and of all the stars. Yet the Babylonians did make many discoveries about the stars; in fact, some of our experts believe it is because of the Babylonians' star discoveries that we count seven days to a week.

Among all the twinkly stars, they saw five that shine with a steady light (we call them planets), and since these were considered rare, they were watched closely. From these observations the stargazers discovered that the planets, like the sun and the moon, seem to move across the heavens.

We know that planets are pieces which have been thrown off by the sun and that they have no light of their own. They shine because they reflect the sun's light. And although the moon is not a planet, it also reflects the light of the sun, and so does our planet, the earth. If we were able to fly thousands of miles into the sky, we might see the earth shining.

The ancient Babylonians thought the five planets they recognized were gods, and one day was set aside for the worship of each. The people of Babylonia already worshiped the sun on one day and the moon on another. Now there were five other gods to honor, and so the Babylonians began to count the days in groups of seven, just as we count seven days to a week.

But how was this custom of old Babylonia carried forward to our world? We do not construct buildings as the Babylonians

HAMMURABI

Wedge-shaped cuneiform writing which was used at the time Hammurabi was king of Babylonia.

did, nor do we dress in Babylonian fashion. Why, then, do we count days by seven?

Many different explanations are given by people who can read the wedge-shaped (cuneiform) writing of the Babylonians and the records left by other Eastern nations, but the correct answer seems to be that our calendar is divided into weeks of seven days because the ancient Jews happened to know about the Babylonian system.

In any event, when the Jews wrote their story of the beginning of the world, in the book called the Bible, they divided time into seven-day periods. Because the Bible became the most important book in the world, most nations adopted the custom of dividing time into weeks consisting of seven days.

Perhaps if the skygazers of Babylonia had had sharper eyes, or if they had had telescopes and other instruments such as our astronomers use, we might have had a week of 10 days, for eight planets can be seen from our own planet, the earth. Just think what a change it might have made in our entire schedule if people who lived thousands of years ago had counted eight planets in the sky, and had dedicated one day to each, in addition to the moon's day and the sun's day. Schools might have been in session for eight days in a row, and grown-ups who work in factories and offices might also have had fewer holidays. If eight planets had been seen, our calendar and our entire schedule for work and play might have been different.

The Lucky Star

IT MIGHT TRULY BE SAID that Imhotep had been born under a lucky star. His home was in Egypt, near the river Nile, and because he was a farmer's son he had to work hard picking cotton, planting grain, and gathering the tall grass that grew along the banks of the river. Still he was lucky, because he had been born on the day when the brightest star in the sky, the one we call *Sirius,* reappeared in the heavens.

In Egypt this event was celebrated with feasts and parties, and Imhotep's birthday was always exciting.

His favorite story was about the star and the river Nile. His mother had told him, as soon as he was old enough to understand stories, that at a certain time each year the star disappeared, and the river-god seemed to know that it had gone, for the water receded until it, too, almost disappeared. As far back as anyone could remember, this had always happened. Then Imhotep's father, and other farmers, who depended on the river to keep their fields moist and fertile, gave presents to the god who was supposed to rule the river and begged him to bring back the water.

Imhotep was always anxious to hear the part of the story about the star's return. He knew that the bright star reappeared

21

early one morning shortly before sunrise and that the great celebration then began. The day was called the beginning of the year.

He learned, when he was still very young, an interesting fact
about the star and the river. One morning he had gone with his
father to a field close to the river, and before starting work
his father had stopped to glance at the water.

"Look, the water is returning!" his father called excitedly.
"Those weeds," and he pointed to the clump near by, "were dry
when we were here last. Now they are half covered with water.
The river is filling again, and soon the bright star will be seen."

Farmers knew from experience that the return of the water
was a sign that the star would soon come into view. They therefore knew when to get ready for the great celebration marking
the beginning of a new year and to prepare for the planting that
followed this event.

Now we know that Sirius, and many other stars, are invisible
for part of each year because during that time they are hidden
by the sun.

Sirius happens to reappear just about the same time as the water in the river Nile reaches the level necessary for fertilizing the ground; the star and the river therefore made a very good calendar for farmers.

The Egyptians did not know that their star calendar was a truly accurate one. Actually, our modern scientists use a similar calendar for their most exact measurements.

But some Egyptian decided that an easier system could be contrived. Instead of waiting for the reappearance of the bright star Sirius, or instead of counting months according to the moon, as the Babylonians did, another calendar was made. Ten days were counted as a week, three weeks as a month, and twelve months as a year.

In one way this calendar was a real improvement. It established a regular system for counting weeks and months. But it was completely unscientific.

It does not matter how many days are counted as a week, or as a month; any convenient number may be used. But no one can decide how long either a day or a year should be. For a day is the exact length of time it takes the earth to spin around its axis, and a year is the definite length of time the earth takes to complete its journey around the sun. These scientific facts were neglected when the Egyptians decided to count twelve of their thirty-day months as a year. Three hundred and sixty days do NOT make a full year.

What was done about this mistake? Simply this: a five-day holiday was declared at the end of each short year. An old man who came often to Imhotep's home told this story about the holidays.

One day the god Thoth, who lived in the sky, played a game with the moon. Thoth won, and as a penalty the moon had to give up a part of her light. Out of this light Thoth made five days, and on each one a god was born. Their birthdays were the holidays celebrated at the end of the year.

This tale was told over and over again. Everyone liked it, and they also enjoyed the five-day holiday.

But even the addition of the five holidays did not provide Egyptians with an accurate yearly calendar. For it takes the earth a little more than 365 days to travel around the sun. To be exact, it takes 365 days, 5 hours, 48 minutes, and 46 seconds. But for a long time nothing was done to add these extra hours and minutes and seconds.

The result was very much the same as if you were to use a watch that runs slow. The Egyptians' official calender kept running slow in comparison with the true sun year. In four years it was slow by about a day; in forty years the calendar was ten days (a full Egyptian week) slow.

If this had happened in the United States, or in any other country with a variable climate, people would have noticed that the calendar was not keeping up with the seasons. But in Egypt the climate is very much the same all year round, so that the gradual slowdown of the calendar was not noticeable.

If farmers had used the slow calendar, there might have been trouble, for then their crops would not have been planted at the right time. But Imhotep's father and all the other farmers used the reappearance of the bright star Sirius and the flooding of the river Nile as their planting calendar. Seeds, therefore, were sown at the right time, and for thousands of years, as far as we know, nobody bothered to make the official calendar accurate. Only long after Egypt had been conquered by Alexander the Great was a decree issued that the calendar be corrected. Alexander's grandson, Ptolemy III, was ruling the land at that time. He was a popular king, but even he had trouble when he tried to make the Egyptians change their system of counting time.

The First Leap-Year Decree

THE KING'S BODYGUARD thought the meeting would never end. The soldiers had taken up their stations early in the morning in the palace at Alexandria, which was Egypt's greatest city, and now it was nearly sunset, yet the meeting was still going on. Now and then the soldiers could catch a word of what was being said; they could hear the voice of the king, Ptolemy, whose nickname was "the benefactor," as he argued with the wise men.

"The king is saying that the calendar must be changed," the soldier stationed nearest the meeting room reported.

"It should have been done long ago," observed the officer who commanded the guard. Sometimes he spoke in a superior manner, because his grandfather was one of Alexander's soldiers who had conquered Egypt and had stayed to make his home in the Nile River country. "We have already enlightened the people a little on calendar matters," he added. "It is now time that further information be given."

He was thinking of the tales his grandfather had told him of forcing the Egyptian scientists to reveal the secret of how the stars could be used as a calendar. These men had made some of their discoveries about the stars by standing outside the great pyramid of King Cheops (this is the largest of the pyramids; it is about the height of a thirty-story building) and sighting up its sloping sides at the sky. From these observations they knew that a star which was exactly over the point of the pyramid on one midnight would reach the same position about four minutes earlier on the following night. They had observed also that the stars that passed over the point of the pyramid seemed to travel the same path in the heavens as did the sun during the day.

The ancient scientists did not know that the stars appear to move because the earth is moving. They thought the stars were boats

that were blown across the sky just as their real boats were blown up and down the river Nile by the wind.

Despite this fanciful idea, the Egyptian calendar-makers did know a great deal about the stars. They could recognize all the stars that passed over the point of the pyramid each year. These stars were divided into groups: All those that passed over the pyramid for thirty days (which was one Egyptian month) were counted as one group, and all those that passed over the pyramid for the next thirty days belonged to another group. Altogether, there were twelve groups, one for each month of the year.

29

Since many of these star groups seemed to form the outlines of animals, one was called the ram, another the bull, another the goat, and still another the lion. Pictures were drawn of this menagerie in the sky, but the pictures were kept secret. Only after Alexander had conquered Egypt were the calendar-makers forced to engrave the pictures in the temples where everyone could see them. They

were called the signs of the zodiac (*zodiakos* is Greek, derived from the word meaning "animal").

After the officer spoke of the star calendar, he asked, "Do you remember the year when holidays supposed to be celebrated at harvest time, according to the official calendar, actually fell due at just about the time the farmers were beginning their planting?"

31

"What difference did that make; we had the holidays anyhow," a soldier said. Another murmured something about the gods decreeing how the calendar should be regulated.

"Keeping an accurate calendar is a scientific matter," the officer declared in a superior voice.

The king was saying very much the same thing to the scientists whom he had summoned to the conference. He himself was a renowned scientist, and he spent at least as much time studying as he did handling affairs of state.

The king knew that the calendar-makers had a rod for measuring shadows and that careful records were kept of the length of the shadow it cast at midday of the longest day of the year (which is about June 21 on our calendar). From these records it was known that the noon shadow on this particular day was not always the same length. One year it might be quite short, on the next June 21 it would be about a foot longer, after another 365 days the noon shadow would again have lengthened by about a foot, and at the end of still another year, the shadow would have grown again. But the next year the shadow would be short again; it had leaped back.

When this happened, the Egyptian calendar makers secretly added an extra day to the year. Thus, every fourth year, according to their calculations, had 366 days. Now the king said that the people must be told this secret.

Some of the scientists objected that the people would not like the change because they were accustomed to counting exactly 365 days to a year. It was because the king listened to every possible argument that the meeting was taking so long. But finally the king insisted that the change had to be made, and before the meeting ended he drew up an edict in which he ordered that an extra day must be added to the calendar every fourth year.

Although this meeting took place over two thousand years ago, we know about the edict because the stone on which it was inscribed has been found. On one side the edict was written in the Egyptian language and on the other in Greek. Both the Egyptians and the Greeks who lived in the Nile country could therefore read the king's order. It was the first official decree of a leap year.

But the scientists were right: people did not want to make any changes in their old calendar. They continued to count 365 days as a year, and after Ptolemy died nobody insisted that the official calendar be kept correctly.

Not until nearly two hundred more years had passed did another ruler issue an official decree about leap year.

The Great
ROMAN EMPIRE

How the Calendar Got Its Name

THE VISITOR was rather short and thin, his clothes were quite shabby, and altogether he did not look like an important person. When he walked into the waiting room it was crowded with handsomely dressed military officers and high-ranking government officials, but as soon as Julius Caesar heard that the little man had arrived, he ordered that this visitor be sent right in; all the others, he said, could wait.

They were old friends, the little man, whose name was Sosigenes, and Caesar, who was head of the country called Rome and of all the lands her armies had conquered. They had met in Egypt, where Caesar had lived for some time after he had conquered that nation. Sosigenes was a famous mathematician, and after the Roman general had returned home and found that his country's calendar was in a snarl, he had remembered his conversation with Sosigenes and asked him to work out a solution.

"To make a perfect calendar," said Sosigenes, "each year must *average* 365¼ days."

At this point, Caesar interrupted his friend. "Fractions of a day do not sound very practical to me."

Then Sosigenes explained that actually there would be no fractions in his calendar; that a whole day would be added every fourth year, making that year a 366-day year, while the three preceding years would have 365 days. Each year would therefore average 365 1/4 days. In other words, he was suggesting the same calendar Ptolemy III had ordered his people to use several hundred years before.

Julius Caesar was convinced the arrangement was a good one, and he decreed that it should be adopted. It is called the Julian calendar, but anyone who knows the whole story might well wonder whether Sosigenes, Ptolemy III, or Julius Caesar should get the credit for it.

If Julius Caesar's order about the new calendar had been obeyed, most of the problems of keeping an accurate yearly time-table would have been solved. But Caesar's enemies stabbed him to death before the new calendar was really established, and then the new officials proceeded to mix up everything again.

For, instead of having a leap year every fourth year, they said that there should be one every third year. But even the plan suggested by Sosigenes was too fast according to the sun — to be exact, each average year was a little more than 11 minutes too long. So when the Romans began to add a leap day every three years, the calendar ran so quickly ahead of the true sun time that it soon had to be corrected again.

Julius Caesar's grandnephew, Augustus, finally straightened things out. After he became the head of the government, he slowed down the calendar by prohibiting leap years until further notice. Then, in the year 8, according to the way we count (the Romans had a different system for numbering years; they counted from the year in which the city of Rome was supposed to have been founded), he decreed a leap year and announced that every fourth year thereafter was to have 366 days. Because Augustus chose the year 8 to begin ·his leap-year schedule, our leap years are always even-numbered years, such as 1948 or 1600.

Augustus ruled Rome for forty years, and during this time many calendars were placed where everyone could see them. One of the popular locations was at the important crossroads and corners;

just as we erect highway signs telling how far one must travel to reach a certain town or city, the Romans erected stone calendars which travelers or people living in the neighborhood could consult.

These calendars supplied much more information than most of ours. Not only did they give the name of the month, and the number of days in the month, but they also told when the equinoxes would occur, those two days of the year when the hours of daylight and night are equal. They told also when the shortest and the longest days of the year might be expected. Then the name of the god who presided over each month, and the religious holidays, were given.

We know about these calendars because some of them have been found in the ruins of ancient Roman cities. They are not so beautiful as many of the statues and other works of art made by ancient people, but they have a fascination all their own.

Even the names of our months are copies of the ones used by the Romans. By the time Julius Caesar started to correct the calendar, the Romans had already divided the year into twelve months, and each one had a definite number of days. The months were called:

Martius	*Quintilis*	*November*
Aprilis	*Sextilis*	*December*
Maius	*September*	*Januarius*
Junius	*October*	*Februarius*

It was Julius Caesar who started the year with Januarius instead of with Martius, for in Rome the state officials took office on January 1, which made this a convenient date to start a new year.

But every once in a while someone would decide to change the name of a month. While Julius Caesar was the head of the state, the name of the month in which he was born was changed in his honor: instead of Quintilis it was called July.

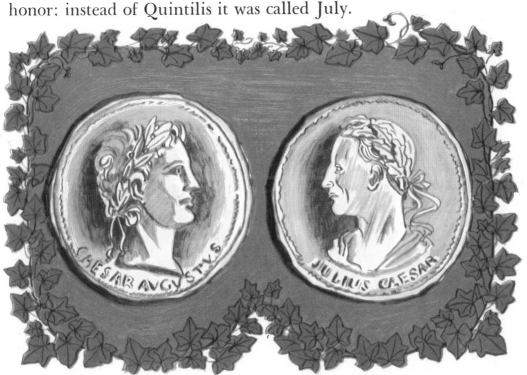

Later Sextilis was renamed for Augustus, and it is said that he chose this month, instead of September, when his birthday actually occurred, because it followed the one named for Julius Caesar. August is certainly an easier word to say than Sextilis, but if Augustus had used his real name the month would have been called Octavius! Augustus means "the illustrious" and was an honorary title that Octavius used instead of his real name.

It is a good thing, however, that we have not copied the Roman's complicated system for numbering days. Instead of saying it was the 1st, or 2nd, or 3rd of a certain month, as we do, the dates had to be given according to the part of the month in which the day occurred.

The first day of each month was the *calends* (which has given us the word calendar). If two Romans were making an appointment to meet on January 1, they would say that they would meet on the calends of Januarius. But if they planned to meet on January 2, they would say: "I'll be seeing you on the fourth before the nones."

In January the nones fell on the fifth day of the month, but in many other months the nones fell on the seventh day, and the Romans had to remember when the nones occurred, because dates

The NONES were supposed to correspond to the moon's

were given as so many days before the nones, or so many before the ides, which were another division of the month, occurring eight days after the nones.

Suppose a school club decided to hold a meeting about the middle of January. One boy might suggest that the meeting be scheduled for the ides (or January 13), another that it be called for the third before the ides (our January 11), while still another might say that the eighteenth before the calends of Februarius (our January 15), would be the best.

Romans always counted ahead — to the calends, the nones, the ides, and then again to the calends of the next month. On statues and on letters and on the ancient stone calendars you can see just how the Romans stated the dates. Our system certainly seems easier.

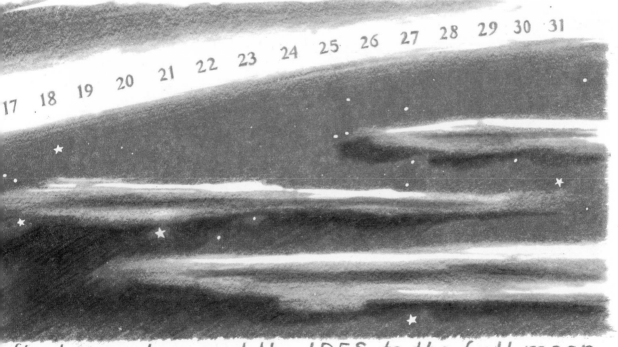

17 18 19 20 21 22 23 24 25 26 27 28 29 30 31

first quarter and the IDES to the full moon

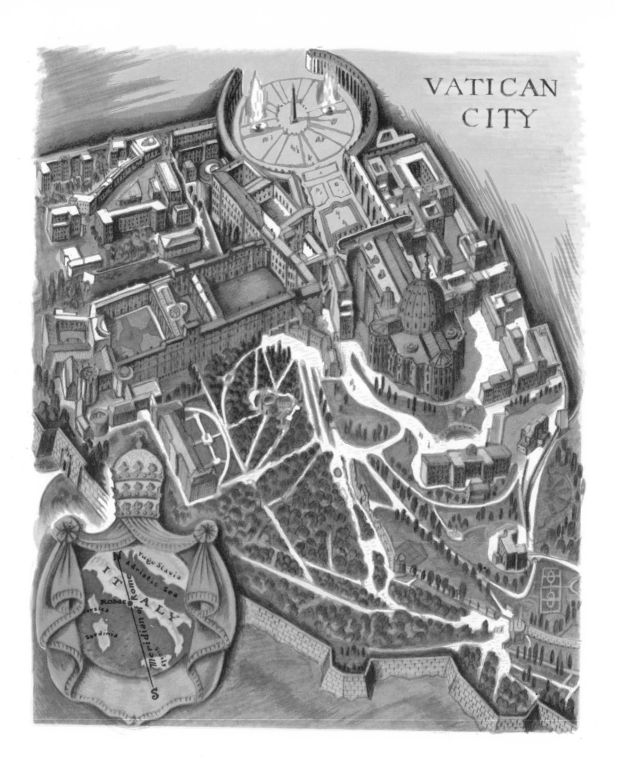

VATICAN
CITY

Too Fast

ONE OF THE OLDEST testing chambers in the world is called the *Sala del Calendaria,* the Calendar Room, and it is located in a building of Vatican City in Rome. This room has a small opening on one wall and a line on the floor, and if you were to visit it about noontime, you would see how the line and the opening were used nearly four hundred years ago to prove that the calendar had run fast.

The line represents the meridian of Rome, or a line which, if drawn on a globe, would start at the North Pole, pass through Rome, and end at the South Pole. At noon, or, as scientists say, when the sun is on the meridian, the sunrays enter through the small opening in the wall and shine on the line.

But each day the sunrays hit a different part of the line. In the summer, when the sun at noon is high in the sky, the rays hit the line close to the wall; in the winter, when the noon sun is quite low, the rays shine much further down the line.

The fact that the spot of sunshine is in a little different position each day was known by the Italian scientists who arranged the demonstration for Pope Gregory XIII. They knew also that there was a certain spot on which the sun should shine on March 21; actually it got there on March 11. This happened in the year 1582,

43

and it proved that the calendar had run ten days fast according to the sun. Sosigenes' mistake of figuring each year a little more than 11 minutes too long had, after centuries, caused the error.

For some time it had been known that the calendar was running fast, and finally Pope Gregory XIII had been asked to make an official correction. It was to convince him that the calendar was incorrect that a demonstration was made in the *Sala del Calendaria*.

After seeing it, the Pope agreed that the calendar had to be corrected, and that a better system had to be developed so that it would not run fast in the future.

It was easy enough to drop ten days from the calendar to make it correct again with the sun. But how was the calendar to be kept right in the future, year after year?

The scientists figured one way, and then they figured another. But, no matter how much mathematics they did, the answer never came out to an even figure. Finally it was decided to continue counting every fourth year as a leap year, but to skip every century year that cannot be divided evenly by 400.

For example, the year 1600 was a leap year because it can be divided evenly by 400. But 1700 was not; neither was 1800, nor 1900. The next century leap year will be 2000. By this rearrangement of the leap-year schedule the calendar was slowed down.

This is the system we now use, and our calendar, named for the Pope, is called the Gregorian calendar. Although it is not quite perfect (it is 26 seconds fast each year, according to sun time), it will be nearly three thousand years before our calendar has run fast by one whole day.

Most countries now use Pope Gregory's calendar, but it took a long time before many were willing to change their old-style calendars. It was one hundred and seventy years after Pope Gregory and his scientists met in the calendar room before the English government corrected its calendar.

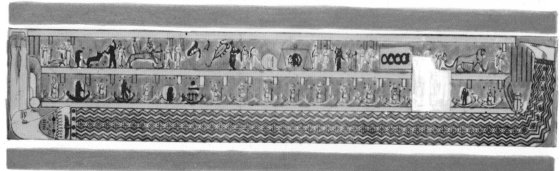

Section of a copy of an Egyptian zodiac originally on the ceiling in the temple of Hathor at Dendera. The blank area indicates a portion which had been destroyed beyond recognition.

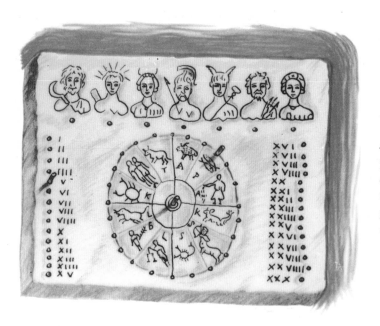

From a Roman stone calendar. The circle, divided into twelve sections for the months of the year, was decorated with the signs of the zodiac. The days were listed at the sides, and pegs were placed in the holes to indicate the month and day.

This was done in 1752, and by that time the calendar had to be set back by eleven whole days. For, in addition to the ten days Pope Gregory had said must be skipped, another day had to be dropped, because the English had added a leap day in the century year 1700. The change was made in September; the day after September 2 was called September 14.

Page from a 1752 American Almanac showing nineteen days in September instead of thirty.

Of course, some people got mixed up, and others were angry about the change. People complained, just as they had in ancient Babylonia when extra months had been added. Families who rented houses by the month, or men who had borrowed money on which they paid interest, grumbled that they had been cheated. They would have to pay the full rate for a month that had been cut short by 11 days.

The difficulty of getting accustomed to the new calendar was increased because, at the same time the 11 days were dropped, a new date was fixed for starting a new year. Instead of March 25, the people were told that the new year would start on January 1.

Obviously, it is more convenient to start a year on the first day instead of in the middle of a month. But why January rather than any other month? Only because Julius Caesar's calendar was the model for Pope Gregory.

When the English calendar was changed, the people who lived in Great Britain, and in the American colonies, which were then ruled by the British, celebrated two New Year's days in less than ten months. There was one on March 25, and then there was the new New Year's Day on the following January 1.

The dates for private celebrations, such as birthdays or anniversaries, also had to be adjusted according to the new-style calendar. To each such date eleven had to be added. For instance, George Washington's birthday was February 11 according to the old-style calendar, but according to the new calendar it became February 22.

Even today the letters "O.S." appear in many books after certain dates. For example, George Washington's birthday may be printed as February 22 (February 11, O.S.). These letters stand for the words "old style," the description applied to the calendar introduced by Julius Caesar and used in the American colonies until 1752. Whenever the letters "O.S." appear, add 11 to the given date and you will have the correct date according to the calendar we now use.

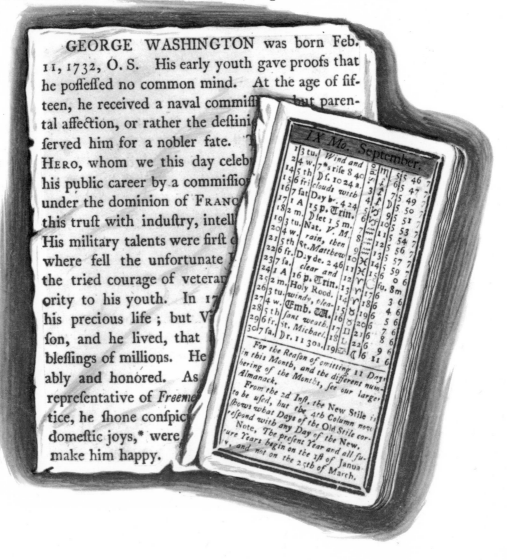

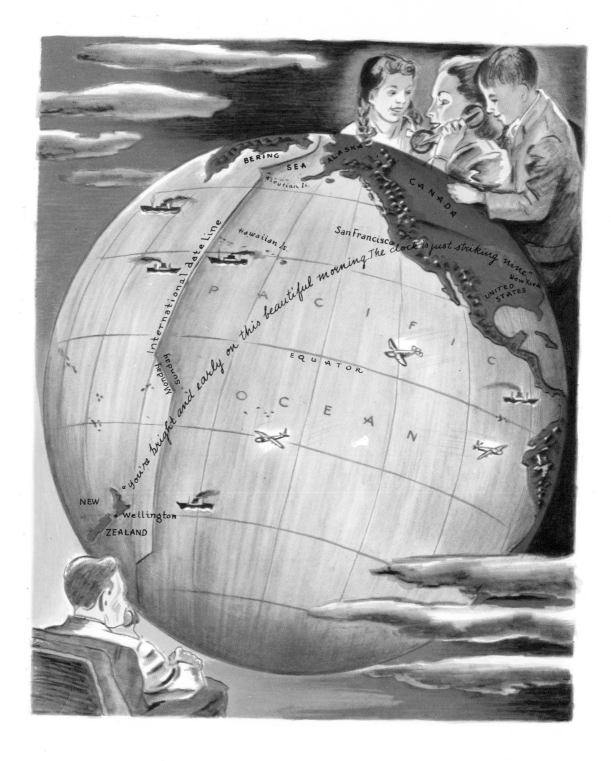

Where Today Is Tomorrow

THE OVERSEAS telephone operator signaled just before 5 o'clock in the afternoon and said that she had a clear connection to Wellington, New Zealand, and the family waiting in the New York City apartment quickly lined up at the telephone; first Mrs. Lee, then John, who was thirteen, then eight-year-old Nancy, for each was to have a chance to say happy birthday to Mr. Lee, who was celebrating away from home.

"Happy Birthday to you," said Mrs. Lee.

"You're bright and early on this beautiful morning," said Mr. Lee. "The clock is just striking nine."

"It's really not your birthday yet," said John, "anyhow, not here in New York."

"We're going to have a birthday party for you tomorrow," added Nancy.

"Well," said Mr. Lee so clearly that everyone in the room could hear, "it's already tomorrow where I am."

The telephone call had been carefully planned to allow for the difference between New York City and New Zealand time. When it was 5 o'clock on the afternoon of May 31 in New York, it was 9 o'clock on the morning of June 1 in New Zealand.

People who travel any great distance east or west in the United States, or to Europe, or across the Pacific Ocean must continually reset their watches to keep them correct with local time. Passengers who fly across the Atlantic to London or Paris must set their watches ahead by five hours in order that they be correct with the time in these cities. When Mr. Lee flew from New York to Los Angeles he had to move the hands of his watch back three hours because it is always three hours earlier in Los Angeles than in New York. During his flight to New Zealand, he and the other passengers had been told that they were crossing the International Date Line and that the calendar date had moved ahead by a whole day.

In the first letter Mr. Lee wrote his family about crossing the International Date Line, he said: "It is an imaginary line even though it is marked on globes and maps. Of course you can't see this line as you fly through the air or sail on the ocean, but it has a very real effect on calendar dates."

The Lee family knew about this imaginary line; they knew that when crossing it from west to east, or, in other words, in the direction from the United States to New Zealand or China, the calendar date is moved ahead by a day; and that when crossing it on the trip back to the United States travelers count two days in a row as the same date, or, in other words, that they gain a day. This line is halfway around the globe from Greenwich, England, which has a master clock and other instruments by which every clock in the world is set.

Nancy had been studying the globe that stood near the window in the living room, and she asked many questions about why the International Date Line was not straight, and why Greenwich had been chosen, and why clocks and watches had to be set ahead or back according to whether one were at a point west or east of Greenwich. They were all intelligent questions, and Mrs. Lee tried to answer them exactly.

Part of the date line, she said, was made to swerve so that it would not cut through certain Pacific Ocean island groups, leaving one or two islands on one side and all the rest of the group on the other side. If this had not been done, the date on one island would have been a day earlier than the calendar date on the neighboring island. The line was bent merely as a matter of convenience.

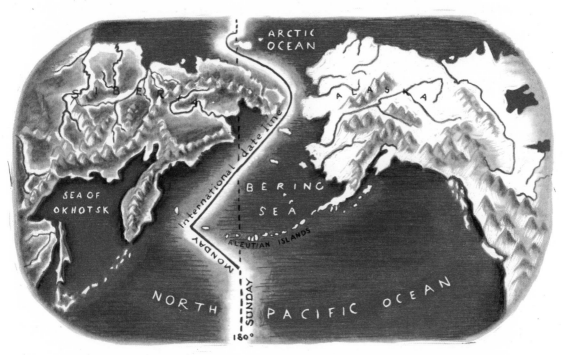

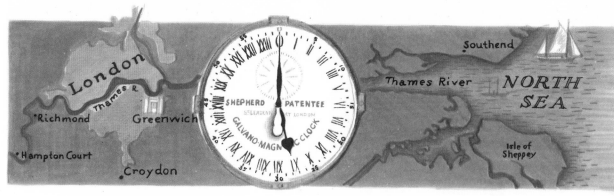

Greenwich, England, was selected as the starting point for figuring time because it has one of the greatest, and oldest astronomical observatories in the world. The observatory was established in 1675 by King Charles II, and the Astronomer Royal was ordered to apply himself diligently to studying the motions of the stars and the moon and the sun and how they could be used by seamen to determine their position when their ship was far out of sight of land. Another duty of the Astronomer Royal was to keep the correct time by observations of the heavenly bodies.

In ancient times seamen knew how to find their latitude, that is, how far north or south they had sailed, by the height and position of certain stars. But they had no accurate way of determining their longitude, that is, how far to the west or to the east they had traveled.

Even when Christopher Columbus made his lucky voyage across the Atlantic, there was no sure way of fixing a ship's longitude. Many methods were tried (one of these was to measure the position of the moon), and in order to get accurate measurements Columbus, and other great explorers, took along skilled astronomers.

For a long time it had been known that if the captain of a ship far out on the ocean could determine the sun time where he was and then compare this with the time at some known place, the difference between the two would enable him to fix his longitude. But working out the solution to the problem did not help much. The Royal Astronomer at Greenwich could supply the exact time in that city, but there was no clock in existence that could be carried on a boat and be depended on to keep time accurately.

Finally (it was in 1714), the British government offered a reward for a method to determine longitude. The most renowned scientists competed for this big prize of 20,000 pounds, (which amounted to about $100,000), but it was won by a carpenter named John Harrison, who made a high-grade clock that kept perfect time even when a ship was tumbled about by ocean storms.

We call such clocks chronometers, and they are set according to Greenwich observatory time. If the chronometer shows that it is 12 o'clock noon at Greenwich, and the navigator finds by "shooting the sun" — which means measuring its height in the sky with an instrument called the sextant — that it is 11 o'clock where he is, he knows that the ship is at 15 degrees west longitude. For one hour of time equals 15 degrees of longitude, because one hour is one twenty-fourth of a day (and night), and one twenty-fourth of the 360 degrees of longitude is 15 degrees.

Since this method of finding longitude was worked out, navigators have always carried chronometers set to Greenwich time. Therefore, when an International Conference was held to determine how time should be kept in the whole world, it was agreed that it should be figured according to the time at Greenwich.

Nancy's brother John demonstrated why clocks must be moved ahead or back according to whether one is east or west of Greenwich. He stood an orange on a pile of books and told Nancy that it represented the sun. Then he started to spin the globe slowly from west to east (the direction in which our planet moves on its axis), and Nancy observed quickly that Greenwich swept past the sun (the orange) before New York, or Boston, or Washington. She saw also that the sun would be visible in these Atlantic Coast cities before it would come into view in Detroit, Chicago, or other cities farther west. In other words, the farther west one goes from Greenwich, the later the sun rises.

Sunrise, and noon (when the sun is at the highest point in the sky for the day) are different in cities even twenty-five miles apart. People once set their watches according to their local sun time, which was satisfactory enough when few traveled far from home and when all travel was slow. But when railroads were built, the differences in the local times became terribly confusing, and it was almost impossible to prepare timetables. The situation got so muddled that it was agreed to fix time zones for the whole world, starting at Greenwich. Each zone is about 15 degrees of longitude wide, and all places in it keep the same time. If you travel westward to the next zone, the time there is one hour earlier, and if you travel eastward, the zone time is one hour later. This system is followed around the globe; an hour is subtracted from Greenwich time for each zone through which one travels westward, and an hour is added for each zone traveled to the eastward. And halfway around the globe from Greenwich the calendar date is changed.

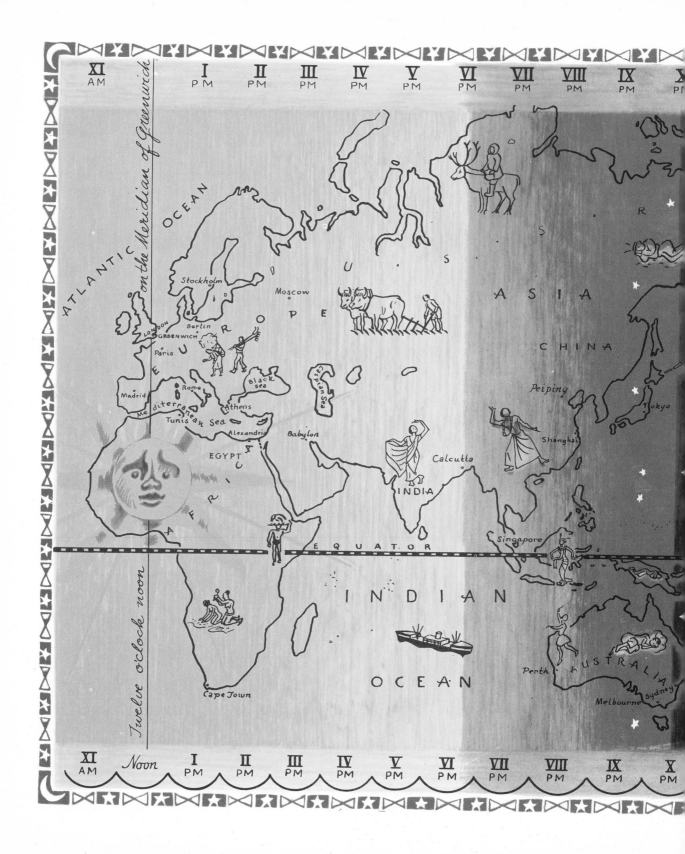

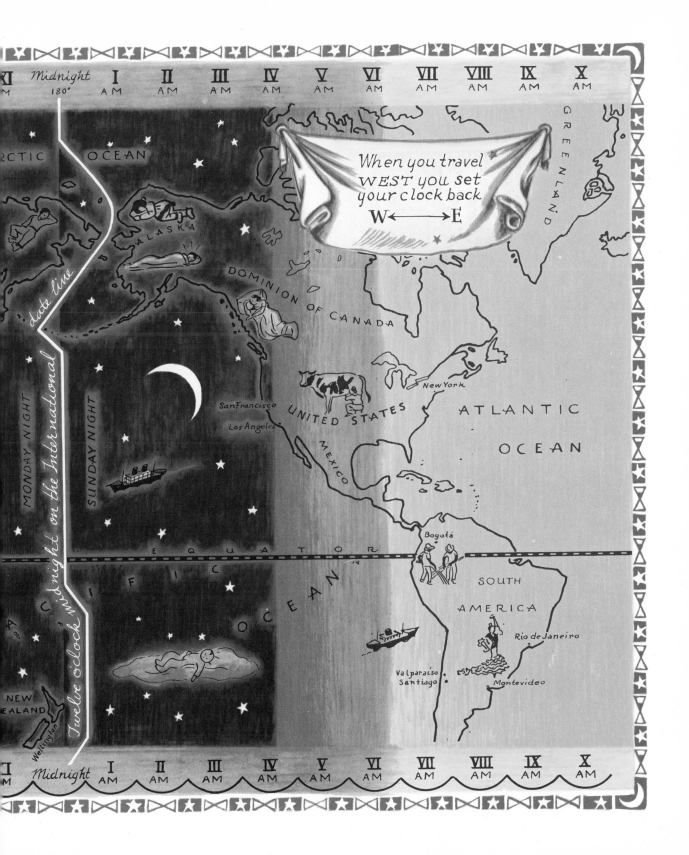

New Year's on Sunday

IT WAS THE FIRST DAY of the new school term, and during the recess a group of boys and girls gathered near the big calendar hanging on the door, and one of them began to look up the days on which school holidays would occur.

"Lincoln's birthday is on a Wednesday," he said. "Do you remember what day it was last year?"

Just then a teacher came by, smiled, and stopped when she saw what was going on.

"It would be easier if holidays always came on definite days," she observed, "and many people think our calendar should be rearranged in this way."

Then she told them of the plans for a calendar, to be known as the World Calendar, according to which New Year's Day would always be a Sunday. And in the same way every other holiday would be celebrated on one particular day, year in and year out.

For example, February 12, Lincoln's birthday, would always come on a Sunday. Washington's birthday would be celebrated on Saturday, the day before, or February 11. In other words, it would be put back to the date that was his birthday until Pope Gregory changed the calendar.

61

In order to regulate the calendar in this way, changes would have to be made in the number of days of the months. These are the changes that might be made.

January would have 31 days, while February and March would each be allotted 30 days.

April would be a 31-day month, while May and June would be 30-day months. July and October also would each have 31 days.

Under this system, there would be four months with 31 days and eight months with 30 days, each 31-day month being followed by two 30-day months.

"We'd need a new rhyme," said one of the boys, "to take the place of

Thirty days hath September,
April, June, and November.
All the rest have thirty-one
Save February alone.
Twenty-eight is all its score
'Til Leap Year gives it one day more."

Then someone else said, "If the calendar were changed I'd have a real problem about my birthday. Other people would have trouble, too. I was born on March 31, but in the new calendar there would be no such date. I suppose, like George Washington, I'd have to change my birthday, too. I wonder if I would celebrate it on April 1?"

"No," said the teacher. "Your birthday would be celebrated on March 30. The system would be exactly the same as the one we now use when a person is born on Leap Day. Except in Leap Years, when there is a February 29, the birthday is moved ahead by a day and is observed on February 28."

Meanwhile one of the girls had been doing some arithmetic. Now she pointed out that four months with 31 days and eight months with 30 days would come to only 364. She wanted to know whether the new calendar would shorten each year by one day.

"No one would suggest doing that," the teacher answered quickly. "Our 365-day year is so nearly right according to the sun that no one would want to change it."

The 365th day would be added at the end of the year, and it would be called a "Year-End" holiday. It would come between December 30 and January 1. This plan is an improvement over the one the ancient Egyptians used when they added five holidays at the end of their short year of 360 days to bring the total to 365.

In Leap Years a second holiday would be added after June 30. This would be Leap-Year Day, and the new calendar would therefore be just as scientifically correct as the one we now use.

Of course, it does not matter to what month a leap day is added. It can be added at any time of the year, in the very beginning, in the middle, or at the end. The important thing is that every leap year must have 366 days to keep our calendar nearly correct. The advantage of the World Calendar system of calling the day after June 30 Leap Day is that it would divide every leap year into equal halves, each half having 183 days.

Many other suggestions have been made for improving our calendar. There was one, for instance, to divide the year into 13 months. But the plan of keeping the twelve-month system and changing the number of days in the months seems to be the most popular. Businessmen would find it convenient because the year would be divided into four equal quarters. It would also simplify planning for holidays, because these would always occur on the same day.

Many nations have already voted for this new system. If it is adopted, a new chapter will be written in the story of our calendar.

21795 9

J
529 B
BRINDZE
THE STORY OF OUR CALENDAR
3.50

DISCARD

York

4